Presentation by *BookLeaf Publishing*

Web: www.bookleafpub.com

E-mail: info@bookleafpub.com

ISBN: 9789357214605

First edition 2022

AF214487

I dedicate this book to my family, who mean the world to me

ACKNOWLEDGEMENT

Thanks to BookLeaf Publishing for the opportunity of taking part in this 21 day challenge, the likes of which I haven't seen before

PREFACE

There are a variety of topics which deal with many types of experiences – some real and some imagined. A few of these are downright silly (reminding me of my childhood), whilst others are similar to everyday experiences, which we can all have or know of. It is intended for adults.

PADDINGTON'S ROYAL INVITATION

We had a picnic tea together -
HRM and I
The Queen of England and little old me
I still don't know quite why
She invited me that fateful day
But we got on so well
And talked together for hours and hours
Of what, I'll never tell

The fact that she kept sandwiches inside her royal bag
Made me realise she's quite like me
Although I shouldn't brag
But nothing will ever surpass that day
I met the Queen, I know
And she has a place within my heart
I really do love her so

THE HOODLUMS

They drove away in a pick-up truck
that day they decided to leave
some teenage boys from the wrong side of town,
who made people cross and made them frown
that day they drove away

They thought they'd have some fun, they did, as
they drove so fast that day
They nearly knocked a woman down
As she rushed to get out of their way

On they went and faster still
That pick-up truck did shake
It went at 80 miles an hour
and made a lot of people cower
Did they even know how to brake?

It didn't turn out very well that day
And they all did come to grief
They were flung from the car as it hit a bar and
excitement, it was brief

Let this be a warning to youths out there
who decide to go out and steal
And drive away so speedily
The dangers are very real

NEW BABY GIRL

Her gorgeous smile and lovely face!
How will her life turn out?
The fact that she's loved is surely the case
Of that there is no doubt

She'll have such fun exploring
As she zooms around her home
Cupboards and drawers are all at risk
As further she does roam

But these things all are normal
And are sure to make you smile
So make the most of this special time
As it lasts for only a while

The teenage years which lie ahead
Are quite another thing
Arguments and slamming doors
Can often be the thing

But through it all, you'll know the love
A special girl does bring
You'll hold her deep within your soul
And your heart, well it will sing

BABES IN THE WOOD

In the woods, the children gathered
under branches hanging low
Gaily calling to each other
Quickly darting to and fro

Deeper, deeper through the forest
They did wander without fear
'til they noticed that their parents
weren't behind them, nor were near

Then they started to feel frightened
What to do, there was no sound
They were lost and it was dark now
Thought they'd better turn around

After half an hour of walking
Crying out and feeling glum
Suddenly they heard their mother
Then they saw their lovely Mum

They did run so quickly to her
Hugged and kissed her once again
Swore they'd never, ever leave her
Stay near house or in the lane

The moral of this story is
Don't run away from Mum or Dad
Everything will be alright then
Nought will happen that is bad

BITCHY GORMLEY

In the town of Bitchy Gormley
Where the blinds do move and twitch
People looking at their neighbour
wondering if they're poor or rich

Everyone is so two-faced there
They all have an axe to grind
Not a happy place to live
But they just don't seem to mind

Then one day two newly marrieds
Move into their house of dreams
Everybody seems to like them
But all isn't as it seems

"Have you seen her cheap old dresses?"
"What about his scruffy car?"
Why can't people be pleased for them
And like the couple for who they are?

Then one day the bride falls over
Breaks her leg then looks around
Who will come to help and soothe her?
But no-one does makes a sound

She is left there, pale and hurting
No one seems to hear her cry
In such pain she can't believe that
She could just be left to die

The moral of this story is
be careful where you choose to live
Bitchy Gormley is the worst place
And a wide berth you should give

THE FOOTBALL MATCH

The fans are in the stadium and the stage is set
There is so much excitement,
Chanting and singing
It's the best day yet

The match begins and each side thinks
 it'll win
They swoop, dive and dodge
Shout "Referee" and appeal
He takes no notice - it's a sin

Then a goal is scored, and things notch up
Happiness for some, misery for others
The same goes for when they tie
The crowd shouts out to support their
 brothers

The agony and ecstasy is how it can be
 seen
They stop for half-time and the manager
 steps in
A peptalk is given and they rush out with
renewed vigour
Both sides are equally keen

The home side gets another goal and the
fans go mad
Only three minutes left
They must hold onto their lead
If they don't, they'll go home sad

So that's it, it's over, they've actually won the
game
Now they can celebrate their victory,
Go out and eat, laugh and enjoy
Now everyone knows their name

OUR LOVELY QUEEN

I knew the time was coming
To me t'was very clear
I did my work up 'til the end
And felt no actual fear

I saw the new Prime Minister
And she was then sworn in
I thought she had potential
And that's why she did win

Now those final tasks complete
I did lay down my head
Then all my closest family came
And gathered round my bed

I think it's then that I did dream
that Philip came to me
He held his hand out, beckoning
And I could plainly see

A bright white light which lay ahead
I just felt so serene
I blew a kiss to family there
And knew that I was keen

To go with him - my one true love
I felt a need to sing
I do hope Charles can manage now
I sang ‘God Save the King”

OLD MAN'S FANTASY

A man and his wife flew off to Spain
To the Costa Del Sol they went
She just wanted to sunbathe, but he had a
greater intent
He wanted to go to a topless beach
And feel that he was young
But when they got there, all they found was
middle-aged people all around
And sure, they were topless but 'twas no joy
For instead of young women they found instead
old pensioners teetering around sun beds
On walking frames which their boobs did reach
The man looked at his wife and said "life's a
bitch"
With a withering glance she replied to him that
she thought they'd feel right at home
They were both 85 and she whipped off her top
and he wished he'd never left home

THE FOOLISH SWIMMERS

They went to swim in the sea they did,
in the sea they swam that day
In spite of all their mum could say
on a cold and frosty winter's day
In the sea they went to swim

They wished they'd done something else, they
did - if only they'd stayed at home
But they didn't want to show they were scared
and acted as if not one of them cared
Oh why had they wanted to roam?

Big high waves came splashing down
Quite scary to behold
But they didn't listen to their mum
They just would not be told

They struggled in the sea they did
As they thrashed around in vain
But then their dad came running down
Determined to save them but wearing a frown -
they'd never go swimming again

So that is how it ended that day

The children were saved from harm
But never again would they risk their life
Their stupidity was certainly rife
That day they did cause such alarm

THE CRABBLE

The Crabble who had no nose
Could neither taste nor smell
And when he went to eat his lunch
it felt just like he'd had a punch
"Twas so unfair when he did crunch
With no taste there to tell

At least the Crabble could hear
And enjoyed a happy song
But when the time was right to eat
He'd sit at the table and eat his meat
But always had to admit defeat
And said not to taste was so wrong

The Crabble stopped eating, which wasn't right
and he became quite ill
We understood how he did feel
How nothing he ate did taste quite real
There was no food that did appeal
He p'raps should just take a pill

So that's what he started to do
He swallowed a pill every day
But the next thing he knew he was ailing
And his body was gradually failing

He made such a terrible wailing
And then sadly he just passed away

LITTLE GORING

In the town of Little Goring
where the owls hoot in the night
Things can often be quite boring
Nothing happens there, it's not right

In the next town, Upper Braying
Women hang their heads in shame
Because of money men are paying
Lots of wives out on the game

Next the village of lower Deeping
Lots of scandal happening too
Booths set up and people peeping
At the naked human zoo

So maybe life in Little Goring
'Aint so bad there after all
Because there is no smut and whoring
People hold their heads up tall

THIS WONDERFUL LIFE

Thinking of my childhood - the innocence and fun we had
Then came the teenage years, uncertainty and angst and yet still the happiness was there
Once I found the man for me, we had a few carefree years together and then started a family like millions before us
Two sons and our happiness was complete

Despite feeling happy, life still had ups and downs
Childrens' squabbles, bickering and fights
Money worries - all of these things are natural and life was certainly not beige
Boys to football, tennis and scouts
So very busy but the best time of our lives
Then they grew up and flew the nest

Our third age arrived, uninvited
We had all the freedom we wanted
And yet we missed our bustling family life
Not only the boys, but also their friends who used to come around for bbq's or just to chill
We gradually got used to being on our own
And holidaying with friends began

Grandchildren then started to arrive
What a very special time and we can share in their life forever
They are all so different as you would expect
And we feel so blessed
Maybe this third age isn't so bad after all
We love our life but never take it for granted
Family and friends - the recipe for happiness

THE BULLIES

The young lad scampered home from school
hoping to escape the bullies there
He felt so afraid nearly all of the time
It seemed like they were everywhere

He didn't know why they picked on him
What had he done that was wrong?
He kept himself to himself for most of the time
and the days seemed to drag – they were long

He thought it might be 'cause he was brown,
that they taunted him mercilessly
But that wasn't his fault, why couldn't they
please, oh please just let him be?

When he got home, his mum was there
(He didn't even know his dad)
But she didn't treat him much better than them –
the boys who made him feel sad

So what was the answer? He didn't know
but he'd heard of a thing called Childline
He decided to ring them that very day
He just wanted to start feeling fine

So he picked up his courage and that's what he
did and they visited the very next day
They realised how hopeless his life had become
and said they would, of course, find a way

The young lad was taken to step-parents,
And he found they were loving and kind
He started a new school the very next week
And no longer felt so undermined

DIRTY SCOUNDRELS

The girl and the landlord had travelled that day
to a beautiful island afar
They thought it so funny that all of their money
was stolen from out of the bar

They made lots of plans as they travelled that
day but not one of them came to fruition
She had wanted to learn how to dance very well
and did now had the cash for tuition

But they should have realised that no good could
come
when their dreams had no proper foundation
He a liar, she a cheat – no-one they did meet
Did take to them across the nation

She wasn't a grafter - her work induced laughter
which wasn't what she wanted at all
She flung herself down with a big ugly frown
and then down on her knees she did crawl

She got off the stage and was in a great rage
What to do now, she wanted to know
Her "career" was in tatters, they had huge
money matters

How quickly it'd started to go

They came back to England and wanted some
jobs, but they didn't have skills they could give
If only they'd worked hard when they had been
young, they might now, a good time start to live

They realised their folly did Nathan and Molly
And knew they had done the wrong thing
They should've saved cash way back in the day
to enjoy the things money could bring

THE DIET

Fasting for 16 hours a day
then exercise, then eat –
that definitely is the way to go
And we'll still feel replete

But what to eat? we ask ourselves
Leave bread and tatties out
No biscuits, cake or rice we hear
But beer is fine or stout

Carbs are the bad boys now we know and fat, we
can enjoy
Think strawberries and double cream
Or bacon - oh what joy

I think we're on a journey now
with food that gives us choice
And if the weight comes falling off
I know WE'LL ALL REJOICE!

OLD MAN

Please don't stop around here old man, watching us every day
Looking and leering at the things we do
Please just go away

Haven't you got a wife at home,
someone who's waiting for you?
If she only knew what you're up to
She'd be quite depressed and blue

"I once had a teenage daughter
and that's why I'm watching you
As she was the age that you are now
But she died and I'm feeling blue

I'm definitely not a paedophile
Or a pervy type of man
I'm just looking back upon my life
And doing what I can"

Oh dear, on hearing the man's sad tale
my viewpoint wasn't the same

I offered my condolences
which even to me sounded lame

We jump to conclusions all the time
and think that we know best
But there are two sides to every story
Things happen which we couldn't have guessed

So the moral of this story is
Be careful what we say
Do not jump in with both feet first
But try to change our way

AN UNHAPPY WIFE

Nobody knew the pain you felt whilst travelling
through your life
You had a husband, that was true but you
weren't a happy wife

He always thought you were cheating on him,
although the reverse was true
He had women calling round at the house
What were you supposed to do?

You never felt you could leave him while the
children were still small
So you just got on with things each day as if
nothing was wrong at all

However, once it was just the two of you,
you knew that the time had come
You looked around and found a flat
And made plans whilst feeling numb

You got a divorce and coped quite well
Joined a club - found a new special friend
Went to a weekly canasta club
And your misery came to an end.

Your ex-husband died a year ago now
You were surprised that you felt rather numb
As you'd never been very happy with him
And what your life had become

But now in the two bedroomed house where you
live, your life is now firmly on track
Now the lockdown has ended, you can go out
more and your happiness can start to come back

THIS SENSELESS WAR

"THE WAR IN UKRAINE IS OVER"
Those are the words we long to hear
But we fear that it's not going to happen yet
It will probably drag on for another year

A bridge is bombed, and supplies cut off
People are shivering as they stay inside
Children in school wearing coats, gloves and hats
and hoping not to see the ones who have died

It is such a senseless, bloody war
What on earth can really be achieved?
So many people have left the country now
And many more are sadly bereaved

What of the people who come over here?
Their lives have been turned upside down
Thousands need jobs and schools as well
across the country - village and town

We see their suffering and want to help
We'll host them, that's the thing to do
If we can lessen their despondency
Our lives will, in turn, improve too

MISSING

Why do things go missing?
Is it always me to blame?
I put my things into the drawer that's in my bedroom, that's for sure
It always is the same

Blasted creams and ointments
Drops that are for eyes
Cold sore treatment and the like
All disappear and take a hike
It's always a surprise

But then I usually find them
And just where they should be
But perhaps covered over and hidden
It should really be forbidden
To lie where I can't see

So I know that it really is my fault
I should learn to hunt around
And not just have a cursory glance
Which leads me on a rare old dance
But be thorough, complete and sound

'TIS THE SEASON

Christmas is coming and excitement takes a hold
Lists of things to buy and do
Traditions, new and old
As well as all the presents to buy
There's baking to be done
Christmas cake and mince pies too
It all is so much fun

But many people find it a chore
And with money in short supply -
I know it isn't easy, inflation is sky high
We need the spirit of Christmas past
Good cheer and lots of grub
Gathering with friends and family
A sing-song down the pub

Appreciating what we've got
Is so important now
When things do get on top of us
There's a tendency to row
So Merry Christmas everyone -
I hope you have a ball
Have fun, enjoy, remember
You don't have to do it all

OLD FOLKS' MEET-UP

(to the tune of "My Favourite Things"

Crackers and biscuits and pickles and cheese
Old men and women, some starting to wheeze
There for their meet-up, it's time for a chat
All different sizes, some skinny, some fat

Chorus
It's a great time - having fun there
And they all agree
Wednesdays are great, it's their favourite day
and they all do love their tea

Some go for sing-songs and some go for talking
Some get a lift there whilst others go walking
Dominoes and quizzes and cards do get played
There's also some crafting where good things
are made

Chorus
It's a great time - having fun there
And they all agree
Wednesdays are great, it's their favourite day
and they all do love their tea

www.ingramcontent.com/pod-product-compliance
Lightning Source LLC
Chambersburg PA
CBHW051748130826
49812CB00033B/1046
* 9 7 8 9 3 5 7 2 1 4 6 0 5 *